Solving problems using logic gates

When designing logical systems, the first barrier is to describe the situation to which the logic is to respond to the logical function and to design the logical system that will perform this function.

Designing a dual-condition lighting system using AND gates

Objective

Design a lighting control system that turns on a light only when both a motion sensor detects movement and it is nighttime. The system should be designed using AND gates.

Components

Two inputs:

- **Motion sensor** (**M**). When motion is detected, $M = 1$; when no motion is detected, $M = 0$.
- **Light sensor** (**L**). When it is nighttime, $L = 1$; when it is daytime, $L = 0$.

One output:

- Light (Light). The light should be turned on (Light = 1) only when both motion is detected and it is nighttime.

Requirements

- Use only AND gates to design the circuit.

Solution

1. Understanding the problem:

- The light should turn on only when both the motion sensor detects movement and the light sensor indicates nighttime.
- In Boolean logic, this condition can be represented as: Light = M $\square$ L.

2. AND gate properties:

Solving problems using logic gates

- The AND gate outputs 1 only when all its inputs are 1. Otherwise, it outputs 0.
- This property perfectly matches the requirement, as we need an output of 1 only when both inputs (M and L) are 1.

3. Designing the circuit:

- Since the AND gate already fits our requirement, the design is straightforward.

4. Circuit diagram:

5. Steps to implement the solution:

- Connect the Motion sensor (M) to one input of the AND gate.
- Connect the Light sensor (L) to the other input of the AND gate.
- The output of the AND gate (Light) will control the light.

Attention. The output voltage levels (from sensors) and the output load (light switch) must be consistent with the parameters of the logic gate.

Explanation of the circuit

Inputs:

- **M (Motion sensor)**: ensures that the light turns on only when motion is detected (M = 1).
- **L (Light sensor)**: ensures that the light turns on only when it is nighttime (L = 1).

AND gate logic:

- The AND gate will output a high signal (Light = 1) only when both M = 1 and L = 1.
- If either M = 0 (no motion detected) or L = 0 (daytime), the output Light will be 0, keeping the light off.

Truth table:

Motion sensor (M)	Light sensor (L)	Light (Lighting control)
0	0	0
0	1	0
1	0	0
1	1	1

The truth table shows that the light will only turn on (Light = 1) when both motion is detected (M = 1) and it is nighttime (L = 1).

Conclusion

This example demonstrates the practical use of AND gates in designing a dual-condition lighting control system. The light turns on only when both specified conditions are met.

Designing a safety interlock system using AND gates

Objective

Design a safety interlock system for a machine that only allows it to operate when two conditions are met: the safety cover is closed and the emergency stop button is not pressed. The system should be designed using AND gates.

Components

Two inputs:

- **Safety cover sensor (C)**. When the cover is closed, C = 1; when the cover is open, C = 0.
- **Emergency stop button (E)**. When the button is not pressed, E = 1; when the button is pressed, E = 0.

One output:

- **Machine operation (M)**. The machine operates (M = 1) when both the cover is closed and the emergency stop button is not pressed.

Requirements

- Use only AND gates to design the circuit.

Solution

1. Understanding the problem:

Solving problems using logic gates

- The machine should operate only when both the safety cover is closed and the emergency stop button is not pressed.
- In Boolean logic, this condition can be represented as: M = C □E

2. AND gate properties:

- The AND gate outputs 1 only when all its inputs are 1. Otherwise, it outputs 0.
- This property matches the requirement directly, as we need an output of 1 only when both inputs (C and E) are 1.

3. Designing the circuit:

- Since the AND gate already fits our requirement, the design is straightforward.

4. Circuit diagram:

5. Steps to implement the solution:

- Connect the Safety cover sensor (C) to one input of the AND gate.
- Connect the Emergency stop button (E) to the other input of the AND gate.
- The output of the AND gate (M) will be the control signal for the machine operation.

Explanation of the circuit

Inputs:

- C (**Safety cover**): ensures that the machine can only operate when the safety cover is closed (C = 1).
- E (**Emergency Stop Button**): ensures that the machine cannot operate if the emergency stop button is pressed (E = 0).

AND gate logic:

- The AND gate will output a high signal (M = 1) only when both C = 1 and E = 1.
- If either C = 0 (cover is open) or E = 0 (emergency stop is pressed), the output M will be 0, preventing the machine from operating.

Truth table:

Safety Cover (C)	Emergency Stop (E)	Machine Operation (M)
0	0	0
0	1	0
1	0	0
1	1	1

The truth table shows that the machine will only operate (M = 1) when both the safety cover is closed (C = 1) and the emergency stop button is not pressed (E = 1).

Conclusion

This simple design effectively uses an AND gate to ensure that a machine can only operate under safe conditions, meeting both specified requirements.

Certainly! Here's a practical example involving the use of NAND gates, including a detailed problem description, solution, and explanation of why this application is important.

Fault-tolerant door lock system using NAND gates

Objective

Design a fault-tolerant door lock system that ensures the door only unlocks when both a valid keycard is swiped and a PIN code is entered correctly. The system should be designed using NAND gates.

Components

Two inputs:

- **Keycard reader (K)**. When a valid keycard is swiped, K = 1; otherwise, K = 0.
- **PIN code entry (P)**. When the correct PIN code is entered, P = 1; otherwise, P = 0.

One output

- **Door lock (D)**. The door should unlock (D = 1) only when both the keycard is valid and the correct PIN code is entered.

Solving problems using logic gates

<u>Requirements</u>

- Use only NAND gates to design the circuit.

<u>Solution</u>

1. Understanding the problem:

- The door should unlock only when both the keycard is valid and the correct PIN code is entered.
- In Boolean logic, this condition can be represented as: $D = K \cdot P$. It is AND function.
- We need to implement this using only NAND gates.

2. NAND gate properties:

- The NAND gate outputs 0 only when both its inputs are 1. Otherwise, it outputs 1.
- Using combinations of NAND gates, we can create AND, OR, and NOT operations.

3. Constructing the AND gate using NAND gates:

Why build an AND gate using a NAND gate? There are four two-input NAND gates in one integrated circuit. Would you agree with me that if all the gates are not used, it is better to use them to build an AND gate than to add an integrated circuit containing AND gates.

To create an AND gate using NAND gates, we need to follow these steps:

1. First, we create a NAND gate with inputs K and P. This gives us NAND_1 = ￢K · P.
2. Then, we negate the output of the first NAND gate by feeding it into a second NAND gate with both its inputs connected to the output of the first NAND gate. This gives us D = ￢(NAND_1 · NAND_1) = ￢(￢(K · P)) = K · P).

4. Circuit diagram:

5. Steps to implement the solution:

- Connect the keycard input (K) and PIN code input (P) to the first NAND gate.
- Connect the output of the first NAND gate to both inputs of the second NAND gate.
- The output of the second NAND gate (D) will be the AND operation of the two inputs, unlocking the door only when both conditions are met.

Explanation of the circuit

Inputs:

- **K (Keycard)**: ensures the door can only be unlocked with a valid keycard.
- **P (PIN Code)**: ensures the door can only be unlocked with the correct PIN code.

NAND gate logic:

- The first NAND gate creates the negation of the AND operation.
- The second NAND gate negates the output of the first NAND gate, resulting in the AND operation.

Truth table:

Keycard (K)	PIN code (P)	NAND_1 (Intermediate)	Door Lock (D)
0	0	1	0
0	1	1	0
1	0	1	0
1	1	0	1

The truth table shows that the door will only unlock (D = 1) when both the keycard is valid (K = 1) and the correct PIN code is entered (P = 1).

Practical application and importance:

Why use NAND gates for this application?

- Reliability: NAND gates are fundamental building blocks in digital electronics, known for their simplicity and reliability. Using NAND gates ensures the circuit is robust and less prone to failure.
- Security: by requiring both a keycard and a PIN code, the system enhances security. Even if one credential is compromised, the other still provides a layer of protection.

Solving problems using logic gates

- Anti-burglary protection: if the inputs of a CMOS NAND gate are not connected to a defined voltage (neither to Vcc nor GND), they are said to be "floating." Floating inputs can pick up noise and undefined voltage levels from the surrounding environment. Solution are pull-down resistors: these resistors connect the input to GND, ensuring the input is read as a low logic level (0) when not actively driven.

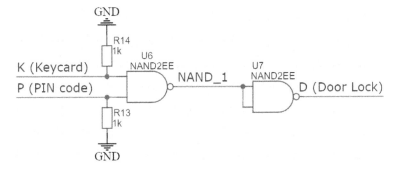

- Cost-effectiveness: NAND gates are inexpensive and widely available, making them a cost-effective choice for designing secure systems.
- Simplicity: the design is straightforward, easy to implement, and can be integrated into larger security systems without significant complexity.

Practical application

This circuit can be used in secure access control systems for buildings, safe boxes, or any area where dual authentication is required to ensure only authorized individuals can gain access. The fault-tolerant design adds a layer of security, making it difficult for unauthorized users to bypass the system.

This example highlights the practical application of NAND gates in designing a secure, reliable, and cost-effective door lock system, demonstrating their versatility and importance in digital logic design.

Certainly! Here's another practical example involving the use of NAND gates, including a detailed problem description, solution, and explanation of why this application is important.

Designing a simple traffic light control system using NAND gates

Objective

Design a simple traffic light control system for an intersection that uses a timer and sensor inputs to control the traffic lights. The system should ensure that the green light is only on when both the timer allows and no pedestrian is detected on the crosswalk. The system should be designed using NAND gates.

Components

Two inputs

- **Timer signal (T)**. When the timer signal is active, T = 1; when inactive, T = 0.
- **Pedestrian sensor (P)**. When a pedestrian is detected, P = 1; when no pedestrian is detected, P = 0.

One output

- **Traffic light (G)**. The green light should be on (G = 1) only when the timer signal is active and no pedestrian is detected.

Requirements

- Use only NAND gates to design the circuit.

Solution

1. Understanding the problem:

- The green light should be on only when both the timer signal is active and no pedestrian is detected.
- In Boolean logic, this condition can be represented as: G = T $\square$¬P
- We need to implement this using only NAND gates.

2. NAND gate properties:

- The NAND gate outputs 0 only when both its inputs are 1. Otherwise, it outputs 1.
- Using combinations of NAND gates, we can create AND, OR, and NOT operations.

3. Constructing the circuit using NAND gates:

To create the required logic, we need to follow these steps:

1. First, we need to create a NOT gate for the pedestrian sensor (P) using a NAND gate.
2. Then, we combine the timer signal (T) and the negated pedestrian sensor signal ¬P using another NAND gate.

Solving problems using logic gates

4. Step-by-step design:

- Create a NOT gate for the pedestrian sensor (P) using a NAND gate:

$$\neg P = P \text{ NAND } P$$

- Create an AND gate using NAND gates:

$$AND\_1 = T \text{ NAND } \neg P$$

$$G = AND\_1 \text{ NAND } AND\_1$$

5. Circuit diagram:

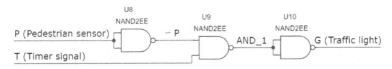

6. Steps to implement the solution:

- Connect the pedestrian sensor (P) to both inputs of the first NAND gate to create a NOT gate $\neg P$.
- Connect the timer signal (T) and the output of the NOT gate $\neg P$ to the second NAND gate to create the intermediate AND_1 signal.
- Connect the output of the second NAND gate (AND_1) to both inputs of the third NAND gate to create the final AND operation, resulting in the green light control (G).

<u>Explanation of the circuit:</u>

Inputs:

- **T (Timer signal):** ensures the green light is only on during the allowed time.
- **P (Pedestrian sensor):** ensures the green light is off when a pedestrian is detected.

NAND gate logic:

- The first NAND gate inverts the pedestrian sensor input.
- The second NAND gate performs an intermediate AND operation.
- The third NAND gate completes the AND operation by inverting the intermediate result, ensuring the green light is on only when both conditions are met.

Truth table:

Timer signal (T)	Pedestrian sensor (P)	⌐P	AND_1 (intermediate)	Green light (G)
0	0	1	1	0
0	1	0	1	0
1	0	1	0	1
1	1	0	1	0

The truth table shows that the green light (G) will be on only when the timer signal (T) is active and no pedestrian is detected (P = 0).

Practical application and importance

Why use NAND gates for this application?

- Reliability: NAND gates are fundamental and reliable components in digital logic design.
- Versatility: this example demonstrates the versatility of NAND gates, as they can be used to create any other logic gate, including AND, OR, and NOT gates.
- Cost-effectiveness: NAND gates are inexpensive and widely available, making them a practical choice for implementing logic functions.
- Safety: ensuring the green light is on only when both conditions are met (timer active and no pedestrian) enhances safety at intersections, preventing accidents and ensuring smooth traffic flow.

Practical application

This circuit can be used in traffic light control systems at pedestrian crossings, ensuring the green light for vehicles is on only when it is safe to proceed, thereby improving safety and efficiency at intersections.

This example highlights the practical application of NAND gates in designing a fault-tolerant and safety-critical system, showcasing their importance in digital logic design.

Designing a simple alarm system using OR gates

Objective

Design a simple alarm system that triggers an alarm when either a window or a door is opened. The system should be designed using OR gates.

Solving problems using logic gates

<u>Components</u>

Two inputs

- **Door sensor (D)**. When the door is closed, D = 0; when the door is open, D = 1.
- **Window sensor (W)**. When the window is closed, W = 0; when the window is open, W = 1.

One output

- **Alarm (A)**. The alarm should be triggered (A = 1) when either the door or the window is open.

<u>Requirements</u>

- Use only OR gates to design the circuit.

<u>Solution</u>

1. Understanding the problem:

- The alarm should be triggered if either the door or the window is open.
- In Boolean logic, this condition can be represented as: $A = D \lor W$.

2. OR Gate properties:

- An OR gate outputs 1 if at least one of its inputs is 1. Otherwise, it outputs 0.
- This property directly matches our requirement for the alarm system.

3. Constructing the circuit using OR gates:

- To create the required logic, we need a single OR gate:

$$A = D \text{ OR } W$$

4. Circuit diagram:

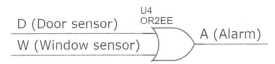

5. Steps to implement the solution:

- Connect the door sensor (D) to one input of the OR gate.

13

Solving problems using logic gates

- Connect the window sensor (W) to the other input of the OR gate.
- The output of the OR gate (A) will be the alarm signal, which is triggered if either the door or the window is open.

Explanation of the circuit:

Inputs:

- **D (Door sensor)**: ensures that the alarm is triggered if the door is open.
- **W (Window sensor)**: ensures that the alarm is triggered if the window is open.

OR gate logic:

- The OR gate will output a high signal (A = 1) if either input (D or W) is high (1).

Truth table:

Door sensor (D)	Window sensor (W)	Alarm (A)
0	0	0
0	1	1
1	0	1
1	1	1

The truth table shows that the alarm (A) will be triggered (A = 1) if either the door (D) or the window (W) is open (1).

Practical application and importance

Why use OR gates for this application?

- Simplicity: OR gates are simple and efficient for implementing conditions where an action should be taken if any one of several conditions is met.
- Reliability: OR gates are fundamental components in digital electronics, known for their reliability and ease of use.
- Cost-effectiveness: OR gates are inexpensive and widely available, making them a practical choice for basic logic functions.

Practical application

This circuit can be used in basic security systems for homes or offices, ensuring that an alarm is triggered if any entry point (such as a door or window) is breached. This enhances security by providing an immediate alert when unauthorized access is detected.

Certainly! Here's another practical example involving the use of 2-input OR gates, including a detailed problem description, solution, and explanation of why this application is important.

Designing a multi-sensor alarm system using 2-input OR gates

Objective

Design a multi-sensor alarm system that activates an alarm when any of the sensors (motion, smoke, or window) detects an abnormal condition. The system should be designed using 2-input OR gates.

Components

Three inputs

- **Motion sensor (M)**. When motion is detected, M = 1; otherwise, M = 0.
- **Smoke sensor (S)**. When smoke is detected, S = 1; otherwise, S = 0.
- **Window sensor (W)**. When the window is open, W = 1; otherwise, W = 0.

One output

- **Alarm (A)**. The alarm should be activated (A = 1) when any of the sensors detect an abnormal condition.

Requirements

- Use only 2-input OR gates to design the circuit.

Solution

1. Understanding the problem:

- The alarm should be activated if any of the sensors detect an abnormal condition.
- In Boolean logic, this condition can be represented as: $A = M \lor S \lor W$

2. OR gate properties:

- A 2-input OR gate outputs 1 if at least one of its inputs is 1. Otherwise, it outputs 0.

Solving problems using logic gates

- We can combine multiple 2-input OR gates to handle more than two inputs.

3. Constructing the circuit using 2-input OR gates:

To create the required logic, we can use two 2-input OR gates:

- First, combine the motion sensor and smoke sensor using a 2-input OR gate: $O\_1 = M \lor S$
- Next, combine the output of the first OR gate with the window sensor using another 2-input OR gate: $A = O\_1 \lor W$

4. Circuit diagram:

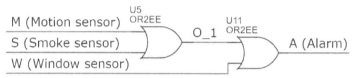

5. Steps to implement the solution:

- Connect the motion sensor (M) and smoke sensor (S) to the first 2-input OR gate to produce O_1.
- Connect the output of the first OR gate (O_1) and the window sensor (W) to the second 2-input OR gate to produce the final alarm output (A).

Explanation of the circuit:

Inputs:

- **M (Motion sensor)**: ensures the alarm is activated if motion is detected.
- **S (Smoke sensor)**: ensures the alarm is activated if smoke is detected.
- **W (Window sensor)**: ensures the alarm is activated if the window is open.

OR gate logic:

- The first OR gate combines the motion and smoke sensor signals.
- The second OR gate combines the output of the first OR gate with the window sensor signal to activate the alarm if any sensor detects an abnormal condition.

Solving problems using logic gates

Truth table:

Motion (M)	Smoke (S)	Window (W)	O_1 (Intermediate)	Alarm (A)
0	0	0	0	0
0	0	1	0	1
0	1	0	1	1
0	1	1	1	1
1	0	0	1	1
1	0	1	1	1
1	1	0	1	1
1	1	1	1	1

The truth table shows that the alarm (A) will be activated (A = 1) if any of the sensors (M, S, or W) detect an abnormal condition (1).

Practical application and importance

Why use OR gates for this application?

- Simplicity: OR gates are simple and efficient for implementing conditions where an action should be taken if any one of multiple conditions is met.
- Reliability: OR gates are fundamental components in digital electronics, ensuring reliable operation for basic logic functions.
- Cost-effectiveness: OR gates are inexpensive and widely available, making them a practical choice for basic logic circuits.

Practical application

This circuit can be used in multi-sensor alarm systems for homes, offices, or industrial environments to ensure safety and security. The alarm system alerts occupants if any abnormal condition is detected, such as motion (indicating possible intrusion), smoke (indicating fire), or an open window (indicating unauthorized access or a safety hazard).

This example highlights the practical application of 2-input OR gates in designing a multi-sensor alarm system, showcasing their importance in digital logic design and safety applications.

Designing a basic SR latch using 2-input NOR gates

Attention! One of the most popular examples often found in exams involving 2-input NOR gates is the design of a basic SR (Set-Reset) latch using NOR gates. Here's a detailed problem description, solution, and explanation of why this application is important.

Objective

Design a basic SR (Set-Reset) latch using 2-input NOR gates. The SR latch is a simple memory storage element that can hold one bit of information. The circuit should be able to set and reset the output based on the input signals.

Components

Two inputs:

- **Set (S)**. When the Set input is active, S = 1; otherwise, S = 0.
- **Reset (R)**. When the Reset input is active, R = 1; otherwise, R = 0.

Two outputs:

- **Q (Q)**. The primary output of the latch.
- **Ō(Ō)**. The complementary output of the latch (always the opposite of Q).

Requirements

- Use only 2-input NOR gates to design the circuit.

Solution

1. Understanding the problem:

- An SR latch is a basic bistable multivibrator, meaning it has two stable states.
- The latch has two inputs: Set (S) and Reset (R).
- The latch has two outputs: Q and Ō, which are always complementary.

2. NOR gate properties:

Solving problems using logic gates

- A NOR gate outputs 0 if any of its inputs are 1. Otherwise, it outputs 1.
- The basic SR latch can be constructed using two cross-coupled NOR gates.

3. Constructing the SR latch using 2-input NOR gates:

- The latch is constructed by connecting the output of each NOR gate to one input of the other NOR gate, forming a feedback loop.

4. Circuit diagram:

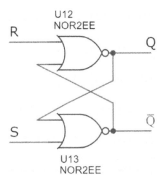

5. Steps to implement the solution:

- Connect the Set input (S) to one input of the first NOR gate.
- Connect the output of the first NOR gate (Q) to one input of the second NOR gate.
- Connect the Reset input (R) to one input of the second NOR gate.
- Connect the output of the second NOR gate (Q) to the other input of the first NOR gate.

Explanation of the circuit:

Inputs:

- **S (Set):** when high (1), sets the Q output to high (1).
- **R (Reset):** when high (1), resets the Q output to low (0).

NOR gate logic:

- The cross-coupled NOR gates form a feedback loop that allows the latch to hold its state.

Truth table:

S (Set)	R (Reset)	Q (Output)	Q (Complement)
0	0	No change	No change
0	1	0	1
1	0	1	0
1	1	Invalid State (Not Used)	

- When both S and R are 0, the latch maintains its previous state (no change).
- When S is 1 and R is 0, the latch sets Q to 1.
- When S is 0 and R is 1, the latch resets Q to 0.
- When both S and R are 1, it is an invalid state for a basic SR latch and should be avoided.

Practical application and importance

Why use NOR gates for this application?

- Fundamental building block: the SR latch is a fundamental building block in digital electronics, used in various memory storage elements and sequential circuits.
- Simplicity: NOR gates provide a simple way to construct an SR latch with minimal components.
- Understanding feedback: this example helps in understanding feedback mechanisms in digital circuits, which are crucial for designing more complex memory and sequential logic circuits.

Practical application:

The SR latch is used in various applications where basic memory storage is required, such as debouncing switches, simple memory elements, and forming the basis for more complex flip-flops and registers in digital systems.

This example highlights the practical application of 2-input NOR gates in designing a basic SR latch, showcasing their importance in digital logic design and fundamental memory storage elements.

Designing an XOR gate using 2-input NOR gates

Attention! Another common example often found in exams involving 2-input NOR gates is the design of a NOR gate-based exclusive OR (XOR) gate. Here's a

Solving problems using logic gates

detailed problem description, solution, and explanation of why this application is important.

Objective

Design an XOR (exclusive OR) gate using 2-input NOR gates. The XOR gate outputs true only when the number of true inputs is odd.

Components

Two inputs:

- **Input A (A).** This can be either 0 or 1.
- **Input B (B).** This can be either 0 or 1.

One output:

- **Output (X).** The XOR output should be 1 if inputs A and B are different, and 0 if they are the same.

Requirements

- Use only 2-input NOR gates to design the circuit.

Solution

1. Understanding the problem:

- An XOR gate outputs 1 if and only if exactly one of the inputs is 1.
- In Boolean logic, this condition can be represented as: $X = (A \lor B)$ $\cdot (\neg(A \cdot B))$

2. NOR gate properties:

- A NOR gate outputs 0 if any of its inputs are 1. Otherwise, it outputs 1.
- Using combinations of NOR gates, we can create AND, OR, and NOT operations.

3. Constructing the XOR gate using 2-input NOR gates:

- We need to create the expression $X = (A \lor B)$ $\cdot (\neg(A \cdot B))$ using NOR gates.
- First, decompose the expression into smaller parts using NOR gates.

4. Step-by-step design:

Solving problems using logic gates

- Create the NOT gates using NOR gates:

  ⌐A = A NOR A

  ⌐B = B NOR B

- Create the AND gate using NOR gates:

  A ⬜B = ⌐(⌐A ˅ ⌐B)

- Create the OR gate using NOR gates:

  A ˅ B = ⌐(⌐A ⬜⌐B)

- Combine the results to form the XOR gate:

  X = (A ˅ B)⬜(⌐(A ⬜B)

5. Circuit diagram:

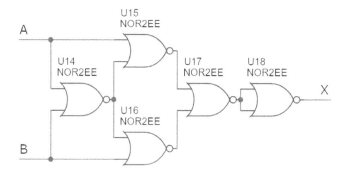

Explanation of the circuit:

Inputs:

- **A (Input A)**: one of the two inputs to be compared.
- **B (Input B)**: the other input to be compared.

Truth table:

Input A (A)	Input B (B)	Output (X)
0	0	0
0	1	1
1	0	1
1	1	0

The truth table shows that the XOR gate (X) will be 1 if and only if the inputs (A and B) are different.

Practical application and importance

Why use NOR gates for this application?

- Fundamental building block: NOR gates are universal gates, meaning they can be used to create any other type of gate, including XOR gates.
- Learning purpose: understanding how to construct complex gates like XOR from basic gates like NOR helps in comprehending the flexibility and power of fundamental logic gates.
- Optimization: in certain hardware designs, using a consistent type of gate (e.g., NOR) can simplify manufacturing and reduce costs.

Practical application:

The XOR gate is widely used in digital circuits for tasks such as parity checking, binary addition (half adders and full adders), and digital signal processing. Building an XOR gate from NOR gates demonstrates the versatility and foundational importance of NOR gates in digital logic design.

This example highlights the practical application of 2-input NOR gates in designing an XOR gate, showcasing their importance in digital logic design and their use in creating more complex logic functions.

Input coupling circuits

In the case of input signals, we very often deal with relatively slow rising and falling edges. Since a gate near the threshold of changing its logical state is particularly susceptible to noise and has a tendency to oscillate, the task of the coupling circuit is to reduce the duration of the edges of the transmitted signal to the values required for TTL systems, while maintaining the noise margin.

Below examples of coupling circuits are shown. The matching of input levels is achieved by transistor circuits, while reducing the duration of the edges of the input signal is ensured by a NOT gate with a Schmitt trigger 64/74132.

Below is an example of a coupling circuit if both circuits are powered by +5V.

Solving problems using logic gates

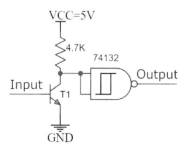

Attention! If the second input of this gate is not used, it should be connected to a driven input or set to a high state (1).

Below is an example of a coupling circuit between two circuits, when one is powered with voltage from 5 to 30 V, and the other is a standard logic gate.

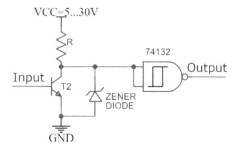

The main purpose of the circuit is to protect the digital input from high voltages and to condition the input signal.

Components:

1. Resistor (R):

- Limits the current flowing into the Zener diode and transistor.
- It is used to drop the voltage to a safe level for the subsequent components.

2. Zener diode:

- Clamps the voltage to a specific level to protect the input of the Schmitt trigger gate.
- Provides over-voltage protection by ensuring that the voltage at the base of the transistor (and thus the input to the Schmitt trigger) does not exceed a certain value.

3. Transistor (T2):

- Acts as a switch. When the input voltage is high enough, it turns on, pulling the input of the Schmitt trigger gate to ground.
- Provides an interface between the input signal and the Schmitt trigger gate.

4. Schmitt trigger gate (74132):

- Provides noise immunity and a clean digital output signal.
- Converts the analog input signal into a clean digital output.

Determining component values:

1. Resistor (R):

The value of the resistor R is chosen to limit the current through the Zener diode and the transistor to a safe level.

Typically, the current through the Zener diode is chosen to be around 5-20mA.

Using Ohm's law, $R = (V_{IN} - V_Z):I_Z$

where

V_{IN} is the input voltage (e.g., 30V).

V_Z is the Zener voltage (e.g., 5V).

I_Z is the desired current through the Zener diode (e.g., 10mA).

for

$V_{IN} = 30V.$

$V_Z = 5V.$

$I_Z = 10mA.$

$R = (30V - 5V):10mA = 25V:10mA = 2500\Omega$ or $2.5k\Omega$

2. Zener diode:

The Zener voltage V_Z should be chosen based on the voltage level required at the input of the Schmitt trigger gate (typically 5V for TTL logic).

Ensure the Zener diode's power rating can handle the power dissipation:

$P = V_Z * I_Z$

For $V_Z = 5V$ and $I_Z = 10mA$

Solving problems using logic gates

$P = 5V * 10mA = 50mW$

Use a Zener diode with a power rating of at least 100mW to be safe.

3. Transistor (T2):

Choose a transistor with a voltage rating higher than the input voltage (e.g., 30V) and a current rating sufficient to handle the input current.

A general-purpose NPN transistor like the 2N2222 or BC547 should suffice.

Summary

This circuit ensures that the input to the Schmitt trigger gate is protected from high voltages and provides a clean digital output, making it useful for interfacing with noisy or high-voltage input signals.

If the information flow comes from contact closures, an RS flip-flop made of two NOR gates, shown in figure below, can be used.

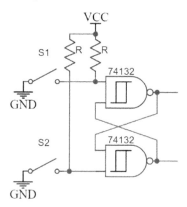

If the input waveform contains high-frequency interference and noise, they can be eliminated using low-pass filters—for example, the simple circuit shown in figure below. The resistance value R in the circuit shown in this figure is limited from above to Rmax≈250 Ω.

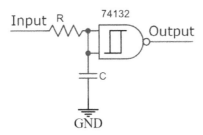

Pulse forming circuits

Circuits that generate a short pulse in response to the edge of the input signal are known as triggering circuits. In these types of circuits, there are no elements with negative resistance or positive feedback loops, and therefore the duration of the output pulses cannot be longer than the duration of the input pulses.

The principle of operation of these circuits involves introducing a delay, causing a temporary maintenance of the high state (1) at the input of the NOT gate, which, when combined with the simultaneous presence of a high state (1) at the other input of the gate, allows the generation of a short output pulse. Figure below shows a circuit that generates a negative pulse in response to the positive edge of the input signal.

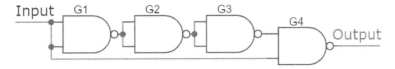

In this circuit, as a result of the transition from low to high state at the input, both inputs of the G4 gate will be in a high state (1) for a short time, causing a negative pulse to appear at the output of the circuit. The width of the output pulse is determined by the delay of the input signal introduced by the three NOT gates (G1, G2, and G3). Increasing the duration of the output pulse can be achieved by adding an even number of delay gates. The delay gates (G1, G2, and G3) can be replaced by 7404 inverters.

Another circuit generating a short negative pulse related to the rising edge of the input signal is shown in figure below.

The occurrence of a positive pulse at the input of the circuit will cause a short period of the high state (1) at both inputs of G1. During this time, the output of this gate will be in a low state (0). The duration of the low state at the output of the circuit is equal to the sum of the propagation times of three NOT gates.

The duration of the output pulse depends on the propagation times of the gates used. Since, in the process of controlling dynamic parameters, it is checked only whether the propagation times of the gates do not exceed maximum values, significant variations in the duration of the output pulses, dependent on the value of this parameter for the used gates, should not be expected.

This passage explains how the timing of the output pulse is determined by the propagation delays of the gates involved, and that these propagation delays are controlled within certain maximum limits to ensure consistent pulse durations.

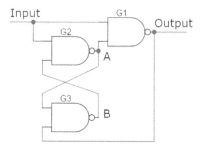

Schmitt trigger circuits

Schmitt trigger circuits are most commonly used to increase the steepness of the edges of input signals in digital devices or systems. The monolithic integrated circuit 74132N contains four two-input NAND gates with Schmitt triggers at the inputs. However, if it is necessary to use NAND gates (7400) in circuits performing the function of Schmitt triggers, the circuit shown below can be used.

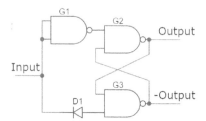

The threshold voltage for the rising edge is V_{T+} = 1.4V and for the falling edge V_{T-} = 0.7V.

In the case of the second circuit the threshold voltage for the rising edge is V_{T+} = 2.1V, and for the falling edge V_{T-} = 1.4V.

Solving problems using logic gates

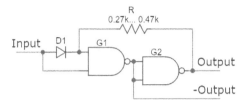

Both circuits are characterized by a similar hysteresis voltage value (approximately 0.7V).

Astable circuits

Figure below shows a schematic of a symmetric astable multivibrator with switching capability.

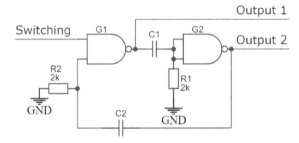

The switching of the multivibrator occurs by applying a voltage V_{IH} or V_{IL} to the second input of gate G1 . A low state at the switching input indicates the blocking of the system, whereas a high state indicates the operation of the system as an astable multivibrator.

For R1 = R2 = R and C1 = C2 = C, the generated frequency value is f = 1:2πRC.

How it works?

When power is first applied, one of the gates (let's say G1) starts with a low output, and the other (G2) starts with a high output.

The output of G1 is connected to C1. This capacitor starts to charge through R1.

As C1 charges, the voltage across it increases.

When the voltage across C1 reaches a certain threshold, G2 switches its state from high to low (or low to high, depending on the gate type).

This change in G2's output causes C2 to start charging through R2.

As C2 charges, G1 will switch its state again when C2's voltage reaches the threshold.

This cycle repeats, causing G1 and G2 to continuously switch states.

The outputs (Output 1 and Output 2) will show alternating high and low states, creating a square wave.

Easy analogy? Think of it like two kids on a seesaw. When one goes up (high state), the other goes down (low state). The capacitors are like springs that slowly push the seesaw up or down, and the resistors control how fast this happens. The switching input can be thought of as a parent who can stop the seesaw from moving by holding it in place.

Key points

Oscillation frequency: the frequency of the oscillation (how fast it switches) is determined by the values of the resistors (R1, R2) and capacitors (C1, C2).

Square wave output: both outputs will show a square wave, which means the voltage will alternate between high and low states at a regular interval.

This circuit is used in many applications like blinking lights, clock signals in digital circuits, and generating audio tones.

www.ingramcontent.com/pod-product-compliance
Lightning Source LLC
LaVergne TN
LVHW022127060326
832903LV00063B/4803